Essential Question
What can traditions teach you about cultures?

The Special Meal

by Paul Mason
illustrated by Courtney Autumn Martin

CHAPTER 1

The Change of Plans

Estela was excited. Today was Vicky's pool party. All their friends would be there.

Estela's mom was unfolding her **precious** tablecloth. It was only used to **celebrate** special events.

"Come help me get ready," her mother said.

Estela frowned.

"Today is Vicky's party," Estela said.

"Our family is coming over today," her mother **reminded** her.

"Do I have to be here?" Estela said.

"I know it's a **disappointment**!" Mom said. "But family comes first."

"You can help cook," said Mom. "There's lots to do."

"I want to see my friends," Estela thought.

STOP AND CHECK

What was Estela's problem?

5

CHAPTER 2

Helping Out

Soon Estela's aunt and uncle arrived. They had bags of food.

"You have **grown**!" Aunt Carmen said to Estela.

Estela looked down.

"Come help me make mole," said Aunt Carmen. "We'll have fun."

Estela thought about Vicky's party. She **sighed**.

STOP AND CHECK

Why did Estela's aunt and uncle bring food?

Aunt Carmen took things out of the bags.

Estela saw chilies and nuts. She saw spices and chocolate. Estela wondered how they could all go into one **sauce**.

"How did you learn to make this?" asked Estela.

"It's a family **recipe**," Aunt Carmen said with **pride**. "I learned it from my mother."

STOP AND CHECK

What was special about the sauce they were making?

9

CHAPTER 3
Making Mole

Estela **crushed** the spices.

"That was my job when I was a girl," Aunt Carmen said. "Making mole is a family **tradition**."

Soon the mole was cooking.
Aunt Carmen gave Estela a taste.

"Yum!" said Estela.

STOP AND CHECK

Why did Aunt Carmen tell Estela that she crushed the spices as a girl?

Next, Grandpa and Grandma arrived.

"That smells good," said Grandpa.

"Estela made most of it herself,"
Aunt Carmen said.

Estela smiled and blushed.

Soon the food was ready. Everyone was happy to be eating together. Even Estela was smiling.

STOP AND CHECK

How did Estela feel then?

13

CHAPTER 4

The Best Part

Mom carried the mole to the table.

Estela watched everyone **spoon** the sauce onto their plates.

"Yum!" said Grandpa.

Everyone agreed.

Estela was happy. This was better than a pool party. She had fun helping her aunt. And now she could make a family **dish**!

STOP AND CHECK

What did Estela learn that day?

Respond to Reading

Summarize

Summarize *The Special Meal.*
Use details from the story
to help you.

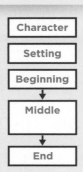

Character

Setting

Beginning

Middle

End

Text Evidence

1. What happened to Estela at the beginning of the story? Sequence

2. Find the word *spoon* on page 14. What does this verb help you understand about mole? Vocabulary

3. Write about how Estela's feelings changed in the story.

   Write About Reading

Compare Texts
Read about mole sauce.

More About Mole

Do you put chocolate on chicken?
Wouldn't that taste strange?

There is chocolate in mole sauce.
Mole has other things in it, too.

Monkman/Photodisc/Getty Images

Mole sauce comes from Mexico. It is a famous part of Mexican culture. Mole can be sweet. Mole can be spicy. There are many ways to make it. Families have their own recipes.

nuts

chocolate

chili peppers

tomatoes

garlic

onion

Chocolate is made from the cacao plant. It is not sweet until sugar is added.

It takes a long time to make mole. First, you get things ready. Then, you mix them all together. The mole cooks for many hours. Finally, it is ready to eat.

Mole is eaten on special days. It is served at weddings and on holidays.

Make Connections

How did reading about mole help you understand Mexican culture?
Essential Question

What Mexican traditions did you learn about from *The Special Meal* and *More About Mole*? Text to Text

Focus on
Social Studies

Purpose To understand how traditions are part of a culture.

Procedure

Step 1 Choose a special food that is a tradition in a culture you know.

Step 2 Make a poster that shows the special food. Show all of the things that are needed to make it.

Step 3 Write a short description of the food. When is it made? How is it made? Explain why it is special for the culture.

Conclusion What did you learn about the tradition of a special food?